# MONTEREY
## PENINSULA

*Photos by*
**ANDREA PISTOLESI**

**BONECHI**

*Distribution by*

**smith** NOVELTY COMPANY

460 Ninth Street
San Francisco, CA 94103-4478
U.S.A.
Phone: (415) 861-4900
Fax: (415) 861-5683

© 1998 by CASA EDITRICE BONECHI
Via Cairoli, 18/b - 50131 Florence- Italy
Tel. 055/576841 - Fax 055/5000766
E-mail: bonechi@bonechi.it     Internet: www.bonechi.it

*New York Address:*
255 Centre Street - 6th Floor - New York, NY 10013
Tel.: (212)343-1464; Fax: (212)343-8045

*Printed in Italy by* Centro Stampa Editoriale Bonechi.

*Text:* Rosanna Cirigliano
*The photographs are the property of the Archives of
Casa Editrice Bonechi and were taken
by* Andrea Pistolesi.
*Photographs kindly provided by* APS *(page 21 bottom),*
Ken Glaser *(Front Cover, page 49 top right, Back Cover
bottom),* Richard Bucich *(pages 5, 6-7, 11, 29 bottom, 32 bot-
tom, 60 top, 61 top, Back Cover top),* Jeff Foott *(page 9),* John
Bryan *(page 10),* Andrew McKinney *(pages 38, 42 top).*

*The "Lone Cypress Tree" and Pebble Beach Property
photographs are reproduced by permission of Pebble Beach
Company, all right reserved.*

**ISBN 88-8029-071-1**

* * *

A bird's-eye view of Monterey Harbor.

# INTRODUCTION

Much as it was in 1602 when Sebastian Vizcaino first described it, the shoreline of Monterey Peninsula is still a nature poem of azure sea, shimmering sea life, white beaches, rocky cliffs, cypress trees, raucous birds and capricious sea animals. At that time, the Spanish explorer sailed into the bay, and upon landing, named the area after a viceroy of New Spain, the Count of Monte Rey, then sailed out again. Bounded to the north by Monterey Bay, to the west by the Pacific Ocean, and to the south by Carmel Bay, the Monterey Peninsula has retained large stretches of unspoiled territory over the 17-Mile Drive, the Del Monte Forest, down through the Point Lobos State Reserve and Big Sur. The remaining area is interspersed by farmlands, vineyards which make notably fine wines, and small communities, each with its own special character.
Echoes of the Spanish past are found on the Monterey Path of History, while the unique sea life and habitats of Monterey Bay are on view in the city's Aquarium. In a twist of fate, the latter is located in a former sardine processing plant on Cannery Row. The New England-style Point Pinos Lighthouse is the prelude to the Victorian clapboard houses of Pacific Grove. The name Pebble Beach immediately conjures images of trim golf courses, golf tournaments, and big prize money. Artists, writers and movie stars dwell in tiny Carmel, where the locals have taken great pains to maintain it as a small village, while some of its boutiques and art galleries are worthy of a big city. On a more spiritual level, Father Junipero Serra's spirit (as well as his body) is serenely preserved within the dreamlike Moorish architecture of the Carmel Mission, also known as the Mission San Carlos Borromeo. Further inland, a mere hop, skip and jump from the Monterey Peninsula shoreline, where it all began, fruits and vegetables are grown in the Salinas Valley – John Steinbeck country.

*Old Fisherman's Wharf is a popular tourist attraction.*

Right: *fireworks at Fisherman's Wharf.*
Following pages, *one gets an immediate sense of history and tradition when approaching Fisherman's Wharf by sea.*

# OLD FISHERMAN'S WHARF

Just as its name implies, Monterey's **Old Fisherman's Wharf** has a long and glorious history.

Its beginnings were somewhat inglorious, as it owes its birth in 1846 to convict and slave labor. But Fisherman's Wharf (not yet old) was soon to play a central role in the history and the day-to-day life of both Monterey and the Monterey Peninsula.

During this initial period, the chief industry of the area was cattle ranching. The pier served merely as a stopping-off point for tall-masted schooners which had circumnavigated Cape Horn to bring food, clothing, furniture and other supplies to Monterey in exchange for cattle hides and tallow. These raw materials were shipped to factories in England, New England, and South America, and were destined for use in shoe and candle manufacturing. In their final form, the goods were sometimes shipped back again for sale to

obliging natives of Monterey! But by the 1850s, economic interests had turned elsewhere – out to sea. Both Portuguese and American sailors discerned a good source of income in whaling. Whale hunts continued in and around Monterey Bay until the 1880s and 1890s. One concrete reminder of the period which still remains in Old Monterey, in front of the Old Whaling Station, is the walkway made entirely of whalebone. Despite its name, the *Old Whaling Station* was originally built as an adobe home in 1847. Eight years later, the Old Monterey Whaling Company established its headquarters there. Employees would ply their livelihood by rendering whale blubber in iron pots on the nearby beach, and at day's end, they would see adventure-loving sea captains dropping anchor at Fisherman's Wharf.

These hardy Yankee souls (in soul at least) were subsequently supplanted by an international group of fishermen in search of smaller prey. This

Today, sightseeing and pleasure craft are tied up at Fisherman's Wharf.

Sea Otter, Monterey Bay.

next generation of seafaring men was to give Fisherman's Wharf its true name. They would sail out in the dark of the night and return during daylight hours, boats brimming with prawns, salmon, albacore, squid, mackerel and rock cod. The crews were composed of Italians (Sicilians and Genoans), Chinese, Japanese, and a number of locals. The Italian heritage of some of the group is reflected in the *Santa Rosalia Festival* held every September, which includes a procession on Fisherman's Wharf, the blessing of the fleet, food and entertainment.

At the beginning of the 20th century, attention increasingly turned to Monterey Bay sardines. Small as these fish are, they meant big business to both Fisherman's Wharf, where they were hauled in, and the adjacent Cannery Row, where they were processed. Then, finally, in 1950, the very last Monterey Bay sardine was canned, and Fisherman's Wharf began yet a new phase of its existence, that of a tourist attraction.

Commercial fishing boats presently dock at the *Municipal Wharf*, east of Fisherman's Wharf, while pleasure and sightseeing craft are tied up at the

*Marina* located between the two piers. Much of the day's catch is still sold at Fisherman's Wharf markets, some of which have been family-run for years. Natives come to buy fresh fish at Fisherman's Wharf, while visitors are usually content to savor the old-time marine ambience as well as a fine seafood dinner in one of the restaurants boasting exceptional views of the Bay. Many feature seafood recipes that have been handed down from one generation of owners to the next. And for those intent on the thrill of catching their own dinner, a fishing trip can be arranged.

An historical note: to the west of Fisherman's Wharf is the site where Sebastian Vizcaino first came ashore in 1602 to claim the Monterey Peninsula for the Spanish Crown. Captain Gaspar de Portola and Father Junipero Serra landed at the same place in 1770; hence its name *the Vizcaino-Serra Landing Site*. Once a sandy beach facing a small inlet, the area was buried under landfill in order to build and widen the present Lighthouse Boulevard. A small Spanish fortress, *El Castillo de Monterey* was built on a nearby hill in

*Above, Harbor Seal in a boat.*

*Right, Sea Lions and Pelicans are the "inhabitants" of Fisherman's Wharf.*

1792, and one can still ascend the summit to see the *Serra Monument*, and to enjoy a panorama of the city of Monterey, Monterey Harbor, and Fisherman's Wharf.

Fisherman's Wharf is also home to shops displaying the meticulously crafted products of local artisans and artists, including, of course, gifts of a nautical turn. Also of interest to the visitor are the occasional arts and crafts fairs and summer theater held in the nearby Custom House Plaza. And on Fisherman's Wharf itself, one can enjoy musical and comedy performances at the Wharf Theatre.

However the lure of Fisherman's Wharf is, as always, represented by the sea. Looking straight towards the horizon, one can appreciate the scenic beauty of Monterey Bay, due in large part to its unique geological formation. Not far offshore is a chasm so deep that it could contain the Grand Canyon twice over. This allows mammals such as whales, dolphins and porpoises to swim closer to the harbor than normally would be expected. During the summer, a phenomenon called "upwelling" occurs; that is, nutrient-rich water from the depths of this sea canyon comes to the surface, flowing into shallower waters around the coast, and providing food for both common and uncommon species of marine life. However many of these species – sea lions, gulls, terns, and pelicans – also enjoy receiving food from human hands at Fisherman's Wharf. The harbor is heavily populated by small harbor seals, large elephant seals, and amusing sea otters, the mascots of Monterey Bay. Once hunted almost to extinction for its thick fur, the protected sea otter now spends most of its time floating on its back, often cradling either its offspring or dinner on its stomach. One can take a sightseeing cruise from Fisherman's Wharf to better view the different varieties of dolphins, porpoises and whales. A particular favorite of whale watchers is the gray whale, no longer hunted. Ranging from 35 to 50 feet in length, it can be spotted in open waters from mid-November through March. During winter months, this mammal is en route to the warm waters of Baja California where the female of the species gives birth, while in the spring, each whale heads home to the Bering Sea. History has come full circle at Fisherman's Wharf.

Above, *the Royal Presidio Chapel was constructed by the first Spanish settlers in 1794.*

Above right, *Casa Soberanes,* below right, *the Old Customs House.*

# OLD MONTEREY

From his ship, Juan Rodriguez Cabrillo was the first white man to catch a glimpse of the Monterey Peninsula in 1542. Although he did not go ashore, the Portuguese explorer claimed the land for his employer, the Spanish Crown. As mentioned, Sebastian Vizcaino and his crew undertook a more extensive exploration of the area sixty years later. Spain, however, ignored his recommendations that the Peninsula be colonized, and it was 1769 before anyone ventured here again. That year Captain Gaspar de Portola arrived overland with soldiers and pack animals, and failed to recognize his destination. After proceeding north to discover San Francisco Bay, Portola returned in the company of Father Junipero Serra, and under an oak tree on July 3, 1770, proclaimed Monterey as capital of Alta California, New Spain's northernmost province. Further inland, Portola built a primitive fort (*Presidio*), enlarged in 1777 with the construction of an outer wall. Most of Monterey's early homes

were located within the *Presidio*. In 1792 the stronghold's weapons were removed to a new fort overlooking the harbor, *El Castillo*. The old fort has vanished, but the early settlement's place of worship remains. The present **Royal Presidio Chapel** was completed in the early 1790s. The small, purely Spanish church, vaguely Baroque in inspiration, is a delight to visit.

Mexico won its independence from Spain in the early 1820s; Alta California became a Mexican province in 1822, and Monterey remained its capital, while the children of the original Spanish immigrants became known as *Californios*. The hide and tallow trade brought wealth to a number of native-born *Californios*, and an upper class was created whose ranks were swelled by American and English businessmen. This group was destined to have an enduring influence on the local architecture. Their homes were built in the form of *adobes*, which combined Indian, Spanish/Mexican, and New England colonial

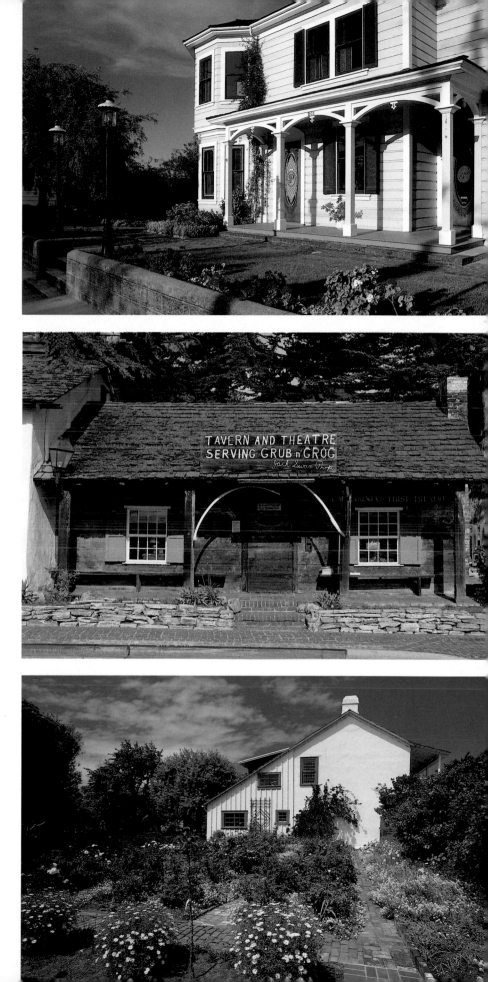

*Left, The New England clapboard style is one type of architecture which characterizes Old Monterey.*

*Above right, the Perry House; middle, California's First Theatre, bottom, the Old Whaling Station.*

styles to produce the serenely beautiful architecture unique to the Monterey Peninsula. The white-washed, mud-brick buildings have a definite Mediterranean flavor, expressed by red terracotta roof tiles, thick walls, and carefully tended walled gardens. The Anglo-Saxons added hip roofs, pane windows, inside corridors and staircases. One example of this "Monterey style" can be seen in the **Larkin House**, home of Massachusetts merchant Thomas Oliver Larkin and his wife Rachael. Another is **Casa Soberanes**, built in the 1840s, often called the "House with the Blue Gate." The interior is decorated with period New England furnishings and items from the China trade. The homes are merely two of 25 adobes remaining in Monterey; some are open to the public, others can be visited either in April during the annual Adobe Tour, or in December, during "Christmas in the Adobes." American residents were also homesick for Anglo-Saxon traditions in a predominantly Spanish culture. Several U.S. Army officers convinced Jack Swan to open **California's First Theatre** in his lodging house and tavern for sailors. Now a national landmark where 19th century melodramas are still performed, it is one of many outstanding historic buildings that can be visited along *the Monterey Path of History*. This walk includes a stop at the **Old Customs House**, where goods arriving in Monterey were unloaded, and custom duties paid to the Mexican government. Construction was begun in 1827; it was completed in its final form in

*Above, Colton Hall, the first American public building in California.*

Top right, *the Old Jail is located at the rear of Colton Hall,* below right, *the Larkin House shows one example of "Monterey style."*

early 1846, just in time for an exciting event to follow. On July 2, 1846, a squadron of three ships sailed into Monterey Bay under the command of John Drake Sloat. On July 7, after verifying that the Mexican War had begun, the naval officer sent an envoy ashore to demand that the military commandant of Monterey surrender. The Mexican army officer handled the matter in an extremely diplomatic fashion. He sent word that all his soldiers would simply withdraw from Monterey. Sloat then raised an American flag over the Customs House and declared "henceforth California will be a portion of the United States." Today, the *Sloat Landing Ceremony* is commemorated annually with speeches, military band performances, and a 19-gun salute. Sloat was not entirely correct, however. It took another four years before the territory was admitted to the Union. In the meantime, the first Chief Magistrate/Mayor (alcalde) of Monterey was appointed in the person of the Reverend Walter Colton, a U.S. Navy chaplain. During his tenure Colton ordered the construction of the first American public building in California. Much to his chagrin, as he recorded, the latter was "erected out of the slender proceeds of the sale of town lots, the labor of convicts, taxes on liquor shops, and fines on gamblers." **Colton Hall** certainly resembled no other local structure. Carefully crafted out of white stone quarried in nearby mountains, the edifice's shingle roof, pane windows, outdoor staircase and porch are New England in style, while its columns and pediments, perhaps a silent acknowledgment to its status as a public building, are pure Greek Revival. Thus the stage was set for California's Constitutional Convention, held in the fall of 1849. The delegates, assembled in Colton Hall, approved the state constitution, simultaneously translating the resolutions into Spanish for the benefit of the eight delegates fluent only in that language, and voted that the state capital should be moved from Monterey to San Jose. The following year California was admitted to the Union as the 31st state. The Monterey Court House was once located at Colton Hall, and guilty offenders would simply take a short walk to their new home, the **Old Monterey Jail**, at the rear of the building. Today, city offices occupy the ground floor of Colton Hall, while the upper floor, its 1849 appearance restored, has been re-opened to the public as a museum.

*Monterey's Cannery Row entered the nation's consciousness thanks to the John Steinbeck novel of the same name.*

*Right, the Spirit of Monterey Wax Museum re-creates the familiar Cannery Row characters.*

# CANNERY ROW

As John Steinbeck wrote, "**Cannery Row** in Monterey in California is a poem, a stink, a grating noise, a quality of light, a tone, a habit, a nostalgia, a dream. Cannery Row is the gathered and scattered, tin and iron and rust and splintered wood, chipped pavement and weedy lots and junk heaps, sardine canneries of corrugated iron, honky tonks, restaurants and whore houses, and little crowded groceries, and laboratories and flophouses. Its inhabitants are, as the man once said, 'whores, pimps, gamblers, and sons of bitches,' by which he meant Everyone. Had the man looked through another peephole he might have said, 'Saints and angels and martyrs and holy men,' and he would have meant the same thing.'"

This image of Cannery Row held true from 1910 to 1950, during the boom of the Monterey Bay sardine fishing and canning industry. This commercial stroke of genius was largely the work of two men, a Norwegian named Knute Hovden, and a Sicilian fisherman, Pietro Ferrante. Ferrante found many of the fishermen, largely of Italian descent, necessary to ply the trade. When Steinbeck's book *Cannery Row* was published in 1945, that year alone saw a quarter million *tons* of sardines hauled into Fisherman's Wharf by huge purse seiner vessels. The multitude of tiny fish were carried to nearby Cannery Row where they were packed in 18 canneries and processed in 20 reduction plants. Hovden opened the waterfront's largest cannery, in operation from 1916 to 1972,

18

*Today, Cannery Row is a popular tourist attraction. The original processing plants are now sites for restaurants, gift shops, and boutiques.*

Following pages, *Cannery Row is inexorably linked to Monterey Harbor's past and present.*

and named it after himself. (As to its fate, see the section *Monterey Bay Aquarium*.) The Row encompassed the entire existence of many of its hard-living residents and workers. They bore the smell of fish by day to emerge and become a part of the cafes, bars and the neon lights of the night; then home to bed to start all over again. Cannery Row had two sympathetic resident observers. One was Ed Ricketts, a marine biologist who collected crabs, starfish, eels, anemones, sponges, and octopi in Monterey Bay tidal pools to sell to schools offering courses in marine biology. He also collected friendships with the odd assortment of individualists living on the Row, and it was the one group he never tried to place in a category. The other onlooker was Steinbeck himself, a native of nearby Salinas, and a qualified marine biologist, one of the many and varied credentials he was to earn in his lifetime. Steinbeck sailed and fished off Monterey in his youth, and immortalized his friend Ricketts as the "Doc" of his novel. The world he portrayed disappeared several years after "Doc's" death in 1948. No more sardines! What next?

Next came the death of old, familiar characters (including Flora Woods, the Row's grand madam, in 1951), the decline of the Row, decay, and, finally, renovation. The canneries, processing plants and warehouses have been recycled and transformed into hotels, restaurants, antique stores, art galleries, and other shops. Cannery Row's past, and Steinbeck's rowdy cast of characters have been re-created in the *Spirit of Monterey Wax Museum*, complete with animation, lighting and sound effects. A sign of how the times have changed on Cannery Row is the wine museum and tasting room managed by the Paul Masson Vineyards. A pioneer in Monterey County wines, this famous California wine producer moved all operations and production to the Peninsula by the early 1970s. However, wine takes up only a brief interval of a visitor's attention on Cannery Row, where a strong sense of the past pervades the surroundings. Although Steinbeck and Ricketts are not around to see it, the Monterey Bay fog still rolls into the Row, where, as well as the buildings, its unique atmosphere has been preserved.

# CONFERENCE CENTER

Monterey also offers the business visitor the convenient facilities of the **Monterey Conference Center**, located within walking distance of Fisherman's Wharf. The attractive three-story structure is designed to accommodate meetings and conferences, both large and small. The *Steinbeck Forum*, a 500-seat theater with a large stage and ultramodern light, sound, and projection systems, occupies the top floor. The two remaining floors contain the *Serra Grand Ballroom/Exhibit Hall* and the *DeAnza Ballroom*, suitable for large groups. Statistically speaking, the Serra can hold 2,500 people and 122 exhibit booths in nearly 20,000 square feet of floor space, while the DeAnza occupies 10,500 square feet, and has the capacity for 1,500 visitors and 60 booths.

The Monterey Conference Center also has a number of smaller rooms which can seat from 10 to 350 guests. The beautiful setting is complemented by large outdoor plazas and terraces overlooking Monterey Bay.

*The well-designed Monterey Conference Center is a popular place to hold meetings and congresses.*

*The Monterey Bay Aquarium houses indoor and outdoor exhibits of the unique Monterey Bay flora and fauna, and it is fittingly located right on the bay's edge.*

Following pages, *the awe-inspiring Kelp Forest exhibit of the Monterey Bay Aquarium.*

# MONTEREY BAY AQUARIUM

The **Monterey Bay Aquarium** is the dream come true of four local marine biologists who wished to share their vision of underwater life with the general public. In the 1980s, they formed the nucleus of a foundation which turned the site of the abandoned Hovden Cannery on Cannery Row into a home for various habitats containing the plants, birds, fishes and mammals of Monterey Bay. How well they succeeded is measured by spectacular Aquarium exhibits and galleries which attract nearly 2,000,000 visitors every year. Live sardines, mackerel and other fish weave in and out of the tall, underwater plants of *The Kelp Forest*, native to Californian coastal waters. It is also fun to listen to "voices of the deep," underwater divers who communicate with onlookers while feeding the fish in this three-story tank. What's out there in Monterey Bay? The answer lies in the deep granite reefs, the shale reefs, the sandy seafloor and the encrusted wharf pilings of *Monterey Bay Habitats*. Sharks cut an

arc across waters shared with king salmon and striped bass; lower down, sand dabs and hermit crabs move smoothly above the sand, while, closer to the surface, dark mussels tenaciously cling to the dock alongside colorful barnacles. Local birds are the subject of the *Sandy Shore Aviary*, which shows a number of species on the move around salt marshes and sandy dunes. Waves come crashing across the *Great Tidal Pool*, inhabited by crabs and anemones among other creatures. This particular exhibit, housed partly outdoors close to Monterey harbor, often attracts visiting harbor seals.
The Aquarium also encourages a hands-on approach at various pools where everyone can stroke the sea star, the black abalone and the sinister-looking yet harmless bat ray. Sea otters can be observed and, more importantly, fed, since these furry animals eat up to 25% of their weight in food every day.

Above, *the distinctive pink hue of the ice plant signals the visitor's arrival in Pacific Grove.*

Top right, *the Recreation Trail leads from Monterey to Pacific Grove;* bottom right, *seals live on the rocks off Pacific Grove.*

# PACIFIC GROVE

There is more to discover on Monterey Peninsula than the town of Monterey and all its infinite attractions. A *Recreation Trail* along the waterfront is a haven for runners, cyclists, and those simply out to take a stroll, and it ultimately leads to the pleasant town of Pacific Grove.

What first catches the observer's eye is the shoreline, composed of tide pools and rocks inhabited by seals and a variety of birds. On the other side of the trail is what appears to be a magic carpet interwoven with hot pink, magenta, and fuchsia colors. In reality, these are the flowers of the so-called **ice plant**, or in botanical terms, *mesembryanthemum*. Besides looking pretty, these ice plants are actually anchoring down the sand dunes of Pacific Grove. Why haven't you seen

them elsewhere in the United States? The answer lies in the fact that the species is native to South Africa. The plant arrived in Pacific Grove during the early 1940s thanks to a kindly and hard-working senior citizen, Hayes Perkins. He uprooted the poison oak in residence and substituted it with ice plants, which he watered and tended for the next 20 years, until the water was piped in and the shoreline turned into a park.

Beyond the ice plants one can observe the area's **Victorian houses**. Built in the late 1800s, their architecture shows no trace of Spanish influence since they were mainly intended as residences for the first settlers, adherents to the Methodist faith. Pacific Grove was established as a

may be visited along the *Historic Trail* or during April's Victorian Home Tour.

Appropriately, Pacific Grove (population 18,000) has retained a small-town atmosphere, ideal for shopping and dining out. It has also remained a wellspring of cultural activity, a position inherited from the late nineteenth century. At that time, the town was the national Chautauqua headquarters. Chautauqua was an institution which provided a series of lectures, concerts and plays, often outdoors, as sort of a "poor man's college." During the period when the Victorian homes were constructed and the Chautauqua lectures were popular, a famous resort came into being south and east of Pacific Grove. This was the *Hotel Del Monte*, whose sumptuous quarters and surrounding park drew visitors from all over the globe. Destroyed by fire in 1887, it was quickly rebuilt and a new attraction added: a golf course! The hotel's success lasted until the 1930s. The

individual house may include gable details, deep recesses and bay windows, outdoor staircases and porches. Pediments are commonly decorated with simple carvings, and the entire building enhanced by touches of wooden filigree, scrollwork, and stencils. All is usually painted in soft, clear colors with white trim.

Some of Pacific Grove's Victorian homes have been converted to bed-and-breakfast inns, often complete with period furnishings, gardens and views of the Monterey Peninsula coast. Others

Above and next page, *panoramas of the Pacific Grove coastline Right. Monarch Butterflies.*

property was later acquired by the U.S. government, which, in the 1950s, moved the U.S. Naval Postgraduate School there from Annapolis. Back to Pacific Grove, one final characteristic decidedly non-militaristic, sets the town apart from all others on the Monterey Peninsula: the **Monarch butterfly** winters there. And not just one Monarch butterfly, but literally *millions* of them. The butterflies migrate south from Canada, generally traveling 80 miles a day, and arrive in mid-October to cover the pine, eucalyptus and willow trees in and around Pacific Grove. They are heralded by butterfly-costumed grade school children who march down the main street to the beat of music provided by local school bands in the *Butterfly Parade*. The orange, black-tipped butterflies seem to take all the excitement in stride. Their main job is to look pretty. After all, anyone caught molesting a Pacific Grove butterfly may, by law, be jailed for six months or slapped with a fine of up to $ 500.

Unfortunately though, when the weather becomes warmer, the Monarchs return home to reproduce, and ultimately to die. Their offspring, following some sort of internal radar, unerringly find their way back. And the cycle continues, and has done so for the last 100 years, beginning shortly after the Methodists' arrival in Pacific Grove.

Top, *The Point Pinos Lighthouse is the West Coast's oldest continuously-working lighthouse.*

Right and following pages, *a quick glimpse of the treacherous coast shows you why the lighthouse was built.*

# POINT PINOS

The sea can be quite rough and treacherous off the rocky coast of Pacific Grove, and ships approaching the area must use the **Point Pinos Lighthouse** as a landmark. Situated on the westernmost tip of the Monterey Peninsula, the lighthouse indicates the entrance to Monterey Bay.

Its beacon has been shining outwards through the darkness and fog since 1855 (Point Pinos is the West Coast's oldest working lighthouse), and has silently witnessed more than one calamity at sea. One of the most dramatic was the 1924 shipwreck of the *Frank H. Buck*. The oil tanker ran aground and, after two weeks, was finally freed from its unfortunate position with the help of spring tide currents.

The Point Pinos lighthouse is also the site of the *Pacific Grove Museum of Natural History* which concentrates its exhibits on subjects pertaining to the Monterey Peninsula. There is a relief map of the land beneath Monterey Bay, including an extraordinarily deep chasm which drops down 8,400 feet below the sea's surface.

How did Point Pinos get its name? When Juan Rodriguez Cabrillo discovered Monterey Bay in 1542 he named it the *Bahia de los Pinos*, The Bay of Pines, and the memory of this ancient name lingers in Point Pinos.

The area and the lighthouse look much the same today as in 1879 when Robert Louis Stevenson showed up in Monterey. The Scottish author had fallen in love with a married American lady, Fanny Vandegrift Osbourne. They had met in Europe; she returned to the U.S., and he followed her, to take up lodging at a boardinghouse in Monterey. Since Fanny could not receive him at first, Stevenson worked on his writings and socialized with Jules Simoneau, who also provided meals for the sensitive individual at his restaurant. Stevenson also spent so much time walking on the local beaches of Monterey, Pacific Grove, and up to Point Pinos, that he was dubbed "the Beachcomber" by the natives. He stopped roaming along the coast in 1880. That year he was finally able to marry Fanny, by then divorced from her husband, and to take her back to Scotland. He left an enduring impression of Monterey Peninsula in his book *The Old Pacific Capital:*

"The one common note of all this country is the haunting presence of the ocean... the roar of the water dwells in the clean empty rooms of Monterey as in a shell upon the chimney."

Above, *a bird's-eye view of the Pebble Beach Golf Links.*

Right and following pages, *the Lone Cypress along the 17-Mile Drive is the America's most photographed tree.*

# 17-MILE DRIVE

The **17-Mile Drive** is a twisting, turning road which encompasses much of the natural and man-made beauty of the southwestern Monterey Peninsula. Originally part of the Mission Trail, the road forms a natural loop. It begins in Pacific Grove, continues parallel to the Monterey Bay Country Club, and then swings along the Pacific Ocean coastline down to Pebble Beach and the Carmel Bay. On its way back, it moves inland and upwards through Del Monte Forest and finally skirts Monterey and, once more, Pacific Grove. There are four approaches to the 17-Mile Drive: at the Pacific Grove Gate, the Country Club Gate, the Highway 1 Gate, or the Carmel Gate. The Drive is famous for its Pacific Ocean panorama which introduces cliffs of sheer rock, seals, sandpipers, cypress trees gnarled by the wind, waves breaking into white foam, and bracing salt spray. The trees, known as the "Monterey cypress," belong to a species peculiar to the

Monterey Peninsula. Robert Louis Stevenson called them "ghosts fleeing before the wind." Poetic description aside, they thrive on harsh conditions by the sea. Emblematic of both the 17-Mile Drive and the Monterey Peninsula is the much-photographed and much-loved *Lone Cypress*, close to Midway Point. According to its signpost, "the largest and oldest Monterey cypress trees in existence" inhabit the *Crocker Grove*. Some of these trees are as much as 500 years old.

The 17-Mile Drive is also close to the home of some of America's rich and famous, and in fact, when driving along it, one is bound to catch a glimpse of the mansions of **Pebble Beach**. This exclusive community has only 2,500 residents, many of whom use the facilities of *six* golf courses in the area. Several of these are set by the water, within sight of the coast.

The world famous golf courses of the Monterey

Top left, *several of Pebble Beach's world-famous golf courses extend right down to the breaking surf along the 17-Mile Drive;* bottom left and top right: *driftwood and stones worn away by wind and waves have created natural outdoor sculptures found along the shore of the 17-Mile Drive.*

Peninsula have hosted many great tournaments over the years. Included are the Bing Crosby Pro-Am and Clambake, now known as the ATT Pebble Beach Pro-Am, and the U.S. Open. The U.S. Open will return to Pebble Beach in the year 2000. The most noteable courses on the Monterey Peninsula are Pebble Beach Golf Links, Cypress Point Golf Club, Monterey Peninsula Golf Club, Spyglass Hill, Poppy Hills Golf Club and The Links at Spanish Bay. These courses, along with many other fine courses located inland from Monterey Bay, make the Peninsula area a primary destination for golfers from around the world. The 17-Mile Drive also offers the beauty of *Spanish Bay*, where Portola and his expedition camped in 1769; the *Restless Sea*, the turbulent meeting-place of several ocean currents; and finally, the **Del Monte Forest**, a part of which is linked with the name of Samuel F.B. Morse, the inventor of the telegraph and the Morse code. Few know that Morse was a painter and a serious one at that. In fact he spent the two years between 1830 and 1832 in Florence, Italy, home of Renaissance art. On his return voyage to the U.S. he applied his talent to a scientific problem leading to the famous discovery which overshadowed his artistic career. Morse subsequently turned up on the West Coast to build the first golf course in California and buy acres of woodland destined to become a protected Botanical Reserve in the midst of the Del Monte Forest. The Botanical Reserve safeguards a mixed and precious group of trees, the Monterey pine, the Monterey cypress, the Gowan cypress, the Bishop pine, and the Knobcone pine, while the entire Del Monte Forest is filled with scented pines and makes for a lovely excursion. In fact, the only complaint one might hear about 17-Mile Drive is the fact that it is a toll road. Keep in mind that money has always been collected along the route, even from passengers traveling in horse-drawn carriages in the 19th century, many of whom came from Monterey's fashionable Del Monte Hotel. Today, one may see people walking or riding bicycles along 17-Mile Drive in addition to cars.

*Yes, one is really on the Monterey Peninsula, rather than Spain or North Africa, as the approach and the architecture of Mission San Carlos Borromeo might suggest. The mission was founded in the Carmel Valley by Father Junipero Serra during the eighteenth century.*

# CARMEL MISSION

Father Junipero Serra seemed destined to follow the Monterey Peninsula trail blazed by Sebastian Vizcaino. In 1602, Vizcaino re-claimed the territory for Spain under an oak tree just west of what is now Fisherman's Wharf. He then proceeded south to discover a river which he named *El Rio de Carmelo* in honor of the Carmelite friars who accompanied him. He then sailed away. Afterwards, the land, inhabited by the peace-loving Ohlone and Rumsen Indians, remained undisturbed by the white man up to 1770. That year Father Junipero Serra, a Franciscan priest, said Mass under the same oak tree where Vizcaino formerly stood, and blessed the construction of his second mission, one of a necklace of missions designed to convert Indian souls.

Serra's primitive mission constituted part of Gaspar Portola's *Presidio*, the original military settlement at Monterey, and military and temporal authorities soon clashed. This prompted Serra to move his activity south, once again following Vizcaino's path, to a lovely site in the Carmel Valley where **Mission San Carlos Borromeo** came into existence in 1771.

The mission's buildings were placed around a cross raised by Father Serra, in full view of Carmel Bay. The early primitive structures were made of wood, but under the guidance of Franciscan fathers, they soon gave way to adobe. Meanwhile, the "Apostle of California," as Serra was later called, founded seven more missions along *El Camino Real*, the "Royal Road," which stretched from San Diego to San Francisco. Then in 1784, at the age of 72, feeling death approaching, he asked for the last rites of the Catholic Church at San Carlos Borromeo, and passed away peacefully during sleep. He was buried here, on the grounds of his favorite mission.

The present mission church was completed in 1797 from sandstone quarried in the nearby Santa Lucia mountains. The architecture is a blend of influences from southern Mediterranean and North African countries. Unusual features include the fantastic star window, equivalent to the rose

Above and top right, *the inner courtyard of the Carmel Mission; bottom left, the church's main altar.*

Bottom right, *the Serra sarcophagus, which is empty, since Serra is buried before the main altar.*

window in European Gothic tradition, and the dome placed above the bell tower, instead of in its usual position over the main body of the church. Perhaps this was so constructed because the interior walls, made of plaster obtained from crushed sea shells, already curve upward in a continuous line to form a catenary arch above the nave. This upward sweep is especially evident at the main altar, which exudes a definite Spanish Baroque feeling. The altar and the adjacent paintings and statues are originals, and these remain in their original places.

The influence of San Carlos Borromeo grew until 1836, when the Mexican government secularized all the missions (a total of 21) and divided their land and cattle between the remaining Indians and the *Californios*, the descendents of the first Spanish settlers. San Carlos Borromeo fell into disuse and semi-ruin until 1933 when it finally regained its standing as a parish church. A dedicated historian, Harry Downie, was put in charge of the necessary comprehensive renovation. In 1960 San Carlos Borromeo was elevated by Pope John XXIII to the status of minor basilica, and is one of only two churches with such standing in the western United States today. A visit to San Carlos Borromeo provides a fascinating glimpse into the mission's natural beauty, art and history. A profusion of flowers, herbs, and palm trees are found in the outer courtyard, while the outline of the church and bell tower is reflected in a pool below the small fountain. The adobe building to the right of the church now houses the *Downie Museum*. Nearby is the cemetery where over 2,000 Indians are buried, their simple graves adorned by wooden crosses and abalone shells. Inside the church, a stone slab in front of the main altar marks the spot where Father Serra is buried. An empty sarcophagus, cast in bronze and depicting the father in a state of repose surrounded by his faithful friends and collaborators, is located in a side chapel. Leaving the church, one can enter the inner courtyard where yet another explosion of flowers and plants is set around a quadrangle containing a pond, a statue of St. Francis, and the Serra Cross on its original foundation.

Above, *the "Doll House" style Tuck Box Tea Room, complete with a simulated thatched roof, is part of the eclectic architecture found in Carmel-by-the-Sea.*

Top right, *more distinctive details of Carmel's architecture;* bottom right, *the soft, pristine sand of Carmel Beach.*

# CARMEL-BY-THE-SEA

Five thousand lucky people live within the one square mile of **Carmel-by-the-Sea**. The town was founded at the turn of the century as an artists' and writers' colony, and many of the current residents are modern-day members of that particular set. In the late 1980s Carmel shot into the national headlines by electing actor Clint Eastwood as mayor.

Eastwood played down his '60s and '70s "spaghetti western" image from a "A Fistful of Dollars" to uphold the sand dollar, the seemingly gentle symbol of Carmel. He proved equally unbending in his new role, and staunchly defended the village's friendly atmosphere and time-gone-by architecture. For this reason there are no neon signs or billboards in Carmel, as these are prohibited by law, and people tend to walk, rather than drive. Thus they can fully enjoy the unusual design of the low-rise buildings, many of which are American reinterpretations of English country cottages.

Gables, shingle roofs, pane windows, flower boxes and flower gardens are the order of the day in Carmel, as are hand-carved and/or hand-painted wooden signs which may advertise unique gift shops, art galleries, dealers in antiques, and clothing boutiques. There is also a discreet selection of gourmet shops featuring local and international specialities, as well as restaurants with European-inspired decor and cuisine. The words "genuine," "sophisticated," "whimsical," "tasteful," and "expensive" come to mind when looking at Carmel shop windows. The town is known as a shoppers' paradise.

Visitors also admire Carmel's beautiful setting. A backdrop of pine trees provides shade for the town, and the Santa Lucia mountains can be seen in the distance. It is easy to imagine why photographer Ansel Adams and poet Robinson Jeffers chose to live here. And, in fact, the latter handed down a landmark to posterity. The "Tor House" is a pile of local stones that Jeffers

*It is clear that many of Carmel's homes and shops were built to vaguely resemble an English style.*

carefully placed together as a residence for himself and his wife, Una. It strongly resembles an 11th century Lombard stronghold, distrustful windows and all, except for the fact that the tower is too short. Perhaps an enemy invasion was not expected; it was probably just Jeffers' refuge from the world.

It is difficult to think of an environment that is more peaceful than this one. Looking like perfect powdered sugar, the white sand of *Carmel Beach* softly flanks the community and leads down to the transparent water of *Carmel Bay*. The sand is completely bare except for an occasional windswept cypress tree. Visitors often come to the beach in the evenings to stroll at the water's edge and to admire the spectacular sunsets. Carmel Beach is also where young and old have fun participating in a Sand Sculpture competition every fall.

Speaking of special events, the town of Carmel is known for its *Bach Festival* which takes place each year from mid-July to early August. At this time the public enjoys a series of concerts, recitals, lectures, and other organized activities. The Bach Festival provides a counterpoint to the annual *Monterey Mozart Festival* held in June. Monterey is perhaps better known, however, for its celebrations of American music. Eight cabarets feature upbeat Dixieland jazz during March's *Dixieland Monterey*, while the blues take center stage in June with the *Monterey Bay Blues Festival*. Finally, to the delight of enthusiasts, the renowned *Monterey Jazz Festival* follows a September schedule.

Other than listening to good music, long and short-term residents of Carmel often take advantage of the many fine golf courses in the outlying area.

# CARMEL VALLEY

"The Carmel is a lovely little river. It isn't very long but in its course it has everything a river should have. It rises in the mountains and tumbles down a while, runs through shallows, is dammed to make a lake, spills over the dam, crackles among round boulders, wanders lazily under sycamores, spills into pools where trout live, drops in against banks where crayfish live. In the winter it becomes a torrent, a mean little fierce river, and in the summer it is a place for children to wade in and for fishermen to wander in. Frogs blink from its banks and the deep ferns grow beside it. Deer and foxes come to drink from it, secretly in the morning and evening, and now and then a mountain lion crouched flat laps its waters. The farms of the rich little valley back up to the river and take its water for the orchards and the vegetables. The quail call beside it and the wild doves come whistling at dusk. Raccoons pace its edges looking for frogs. It's everything a river should be."

So John Steinbeck described the Carmel River and **Carmel River Valley** of the 1940s in his book *Cannery Row*. Today the area has essentially maintained its agreeable rural character, composed of farms and vineyards against the backdrop of the Santa Lucia mountains. The air is clean, and 75% of the days are sunny. These conditions encourage outdoor activities such as golfing, hiking, tennis and riding. Carmel Valley

*Farms and ranches complement the natural setting of the Carmel Valley.*

is especially known for its riding stables, a visitors' attraction. The local climate – warm days, cool nights, and overall moderate temperatures – provide ideal conditions and a long growing season for grapes here and on the rest of the Monterey Peninsula. This fact was only recognized in the 1960s, so local vintners were immediately able to adopt the latest scientific technology without overlooking traditional methods. Carmel Valley vineyards favor the French Chardonnay, Cabernet Sauvignon and German Johnnisberg Riesling grape varieties, and guests are welcome to tour area wineries and observe wine-making procedures. One that offers tastings is the *Chateau Julien Wine Estate*, a Carmel Valley Road landmark which produces three distinct Chardonnays. As its name implies, the estate's architecture is in the style of a French chateau. The *Joullian Vineyards* could be another stop-off for the visitor. Joullian wines are known for their extended bottle aging, which brings out the bouquet and an extra smoothness.

Good food usually accompanies fine wines, and a mélange of restaurants call the Carmel Valley home. One may choose from French, Italian, Japanese, Chinese and Mexican cooking and after dinner, listen to live music or go dancing. Speaking of the performing arts, the *Hidden Valley Music Seminars* are held in the Carmel Valley, with year-round programs of drama, musicals, opera, and chamber music.

*The mild climate and clean air of the Carmel Valley makes it a fine place for the pursuit of sports, including golf and tennis.*

Right: *the Carmel Valley produces some of California's finest wines.*

*China Cove, one of the few spots one can go swimming in Point Lobos.*

# POINT LOBOS

That **Point Lobos** lends itself to the imagination is demonstrated by the fact that Robert Louis Stevenson used its topography as the background for *Treasure Island*. The scenery is unique and, fortunately, the area became part of the national park system in 1933. It was designated a state reserve and attracts 300,000 visitors each year. Artist Francis McComas once called Point Lobos "the greatest meeting of land and water in the world" and one can certainly see why. The area is characterized by startling, craggy rock formations worn away by the sea to form small islands, inlets, and beach coves. Sea lions inhabit many of the outlying rocks. Their raucous barking gave the place its name, since the Spaniards called it "Punta de los Lobos Marinos," or "Point of the Sea Wolves." Just as it does along the 17-Mile Drive, the Monterey cypress clings tenaciously to the cliffs for it requires a moist, cool sea breeze in order to live. The reserve is also a protected area for the Monterey pine and the Coast live oak. Visitors have a choice of trails to follow when exploring Point Lobos: the Cypress Grove Trail, the Sea Lion Point Trail, the Bird Island Trail, the North Shore Trail, and the Whaler Knot Trail are but a few. One can see Carmel Beach, Mission San Carlos Borromeo, and Pebble Beach from an outcrop along the Granite Point Trail. In the spring and summer colorful varieties of wildflowers can be seen along the Carmelo Meadow Trail. A special treat is watching the gray whale spout and dive off the coast between December and May. The water off Point Lobos is cold and clean, and visitors are drawn to the exquisite handkerchief-size sandy beaches of *Gibson Beach and China Cove*; the beauty of the latter is enhanced by hanging gardens. Finally, experienced divers may obtain permission to explore a portion of the designated underwater reserve at Whalers Cove.

*The savage beauty of Big Sur.*

*Pages 58-59, the Bixby Bridge, a Big Sur landmark.*

# BIG SUR

"A walk on the wild side." This phrase from a famous song aptly describes the 90-mile stretch of coastline from Carmel to San Simeon known as **Big Sur**.

Here the Santa Lucia mountains meet the Pacific Ocean with breath-taking cliffs dropping as much as 1,000 feet to mainly rocky coast. There are no villages or cities in Big Sur. Its natural beauty can be explored on foot or by driving along the twists and turns of *Highway One*. Completed in 1937, this road was declared the country's first Scenic Highway by Lady Bird Johnson in 1966.

The area has remained unspoiled throughout its history. In the 1830s, the Mexican government awarded land grants in Big Sur to two of its citizens who later decided not to settle there. A few pioneers arrived during the 1870s and 1880s, and earned their living by mining or cutting redwood timber. Supplies were brought in by ship, and by 1889 the treacherous coastline was

illuminated by the *Point Sur Lighthouse Station*. Another man-made addition to the landscape is the *Bixby Creek Bridge*, which extends 714 feet across the Bixby Canyon. Apart from these structures, the presence of man in Big Sur is limited to some private homes and a small number of guests who frequent seaside hotels and lodges, restaurants, and art galleries. People also come to enjoy camping, fishing and backpacking in the wilderness, and to admire the wildlife. Big Sur hosts colonies of sea lions, sea otters, and a medley of birds. Also located in Big Sur are the hiking trails and hardwood trees of *Pfeiffer State Park*, a nature reserve named after an early settler.

Finally, there is the grandiose castle at *San Simeon* belonging to the Hearst family. The castle architecture is not typical of Big Sur which, in the words of Junipero Serra, remains *el pais grande del sur*, "the big country of the south."

# WILDLIFE

As mentioned, harbor seals and sea lions abound on the Monterey Peninsula, as do sea otters, who possess a valuable coat of fur, thankfully protected from hunters. Off Big Sur, the sea otter lives in kelp beds, the species' natural habitat. Along the coast, Big Sur is a sanctuary for the screeching sea gull, the California brown pelican, the red-billed oystercatcher, and the long-necked, black cormorant, while inland, the red-tail hawk is a common sight, along with the golden eagle, valley quail, and the kingfisher. The lucky visitor might also spot deer, raccoons, and squirrels. At Point Lobos, animal lovers can enjoy viewing many of the same fauna.

Many places along the Big Sur Coast and including Point-Lobos State Reserve, afford the opportunity to observe the whale migration.

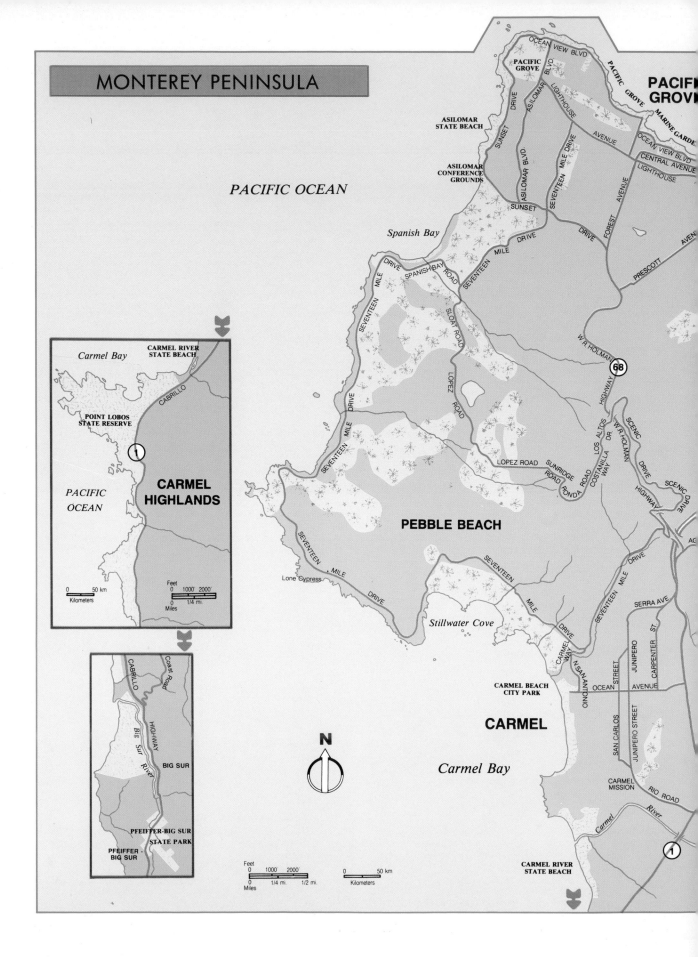

# MONTEREY PENINSULA

PACIFIC OCEAN

OCEAN VIEW BLVD

PACIFIC GROVE

ASILOMAR BLVD

LIGHTHOUSE

PACIFIC GROVE

MARINE GARDE...

ASILOMAR
STATE BEACH

SUNSET DRIVE

ASILOMAR BLVD

SEVENTEEN MILE DRIVE

AVENUE

OCEAN VIEW BLVD

CENTRAL AVENUE

LIGHTHOUSE

ASILOMAR
CONFERENCE
GROUNDS

SUNSET

FOREST AVENUE

DRIVE

DRIVE

PRESCOTT

AVEN...

Spanish Bay

SEVENTEEN MILE DRIVE

SPANISH BAY ROAD

SEVENTEEN MILE

SLOAT ROAD

W R HOLMAN

68

Carmel Bay

CARMEL RIVER
STATE BEACH

CABRILLO

POINT LOBOS
STATE RESERVE

1

PACIFIC
OCEAN

CARMEL
HIGHLANDS

SEVENTEEN MILE DRIVE

SEVENTEEN MILE

DRIVE

LOPEZ ROAD

LOPEZ ROAD

SUNRIDGE ROAD

RONDA

LOS ALTOS ROAD

COSTANILLA WAY

W R HOLMAN

HIGHWAY

SCENIC DRIVE

SCENIC DRIVE

PEBBLE BEACH

Feet
0      1000'  2000'
0      1/4 mi.
Miles

0      50 km
Kilometers

Lone Cypress

SEVENTEEN MILE DRIVE

SEVENTEEN MILE DRIVE

Stillwater Cove

CARMEL WAY

SEVENTEEN MILE DRIVE

SERRA AVE.

JUNIPERO AVENUE

CARPENTER ST

N SAN ANTONIO

OCEAN STREET

CARMEL BEACH
CITY PARK

CARMEL

Carmel Bay

SAN CARLOS

JUNIPERO STREET

CABRILLO

Coast Road

Big Sur River

HIGHWAY

BIG SUR

PFEIFFER-BIG SUR
STATE PARK

PFEIFFER -
BIG SUR

N

CARMEL
MISSION

RIO ROAD

Carmel River

Feet
0      1000'  2000'
0      1/4 mi.   1/2 mi.
Miles

0      50 km
Kilometers

CARMEL RIVER
STATE BEACH

1

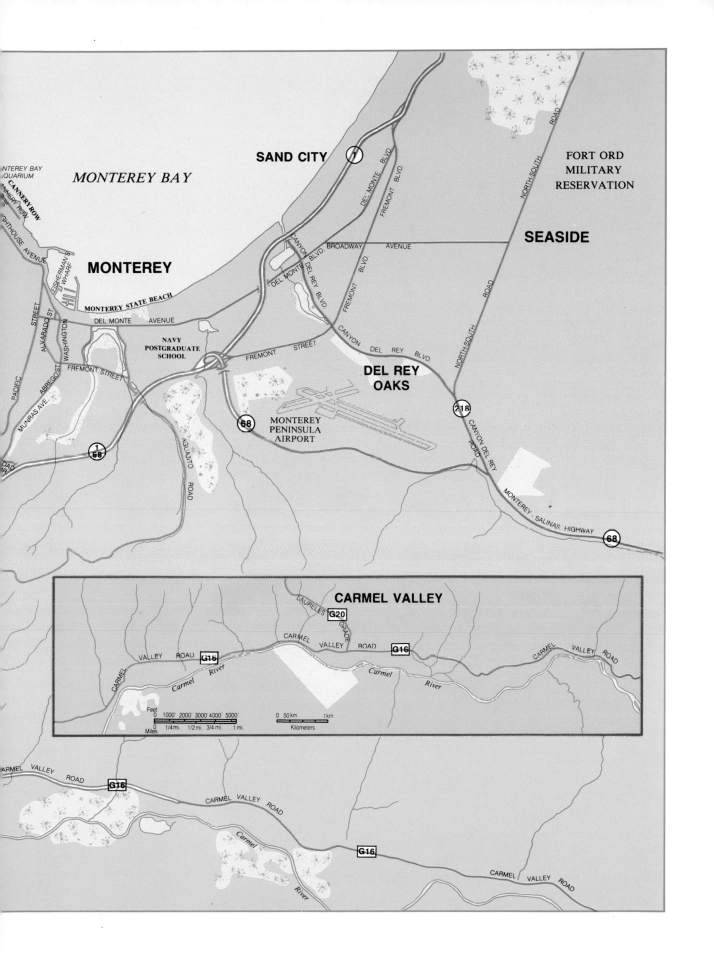

# INDEX